Academic Speaking and the Boundaries of Routinized Lexical Phrases

Academic Speaking and the Boundaries of Routinized Lexical Phrases

Best of Michigan

Susan M. Barone, Ph.D.
Director, Senior Lecturer
Vanderbilt University

&

Summer Dickinson, Ph.D.
ESL Team Lead
Smyrna Primary School

University of Michigan Press
Ann Arbor

First paperback edition 2023

An earlier version of this material was published in a chapter in *Understanding the Courses We Teach: Local Perspectives on English Language Teaching*, edited by John Murphy and Patricia Byrd (copyright 2001).

Published in the United States of America by the
University of Michigan Press

First published April 2022

The presentation of tables, figures, and/or images is dependent on the device and display options. Some image content or language characters may have been removed or may be altered depending on the device used to read this Brief Instructional Guide.

Paperback ISBN: 978-0-472-03943-2
Ebook ISBN: 978-0-472-12735-1

CONTENTS

Introduction

In 2001, Graham and Barone outlined an academic speaking course in the book *Understanding the Courses We Teach* (Murphy & Byrd, 2001). The chapter homed in on the use of formulaic lexical phrases, or commonly used academic multi-word phrases such as *to begin with* and *the x axis represents* to support students taking longer turns while speaking in an academic setting. Now, 20 years later, Barone and Dickinson revisit the concepts and practices of this English for Academic Purposes (EAP) course and reflect on how more recent research and classroom practices have informed and shaped current iterations. This Brief Instructional Guide takes a broader approach to discussing this academic speaking course than the original while also providing English language instructors with relevant approaches and strategies for teaching conventional, formulaic lexical phrases in academic settings.

As we know, teaching lexical phrases can expose students to the language used within university courses and academic environments. Often, the challenge is creating authentic, realistic, and discipline-specific classroom environments that simulate aspects of their academic and research-related contexts.

While this short Brief Instructional Guide provides ideas on teaching academic lexical phrases, we find it important to address other questions related to how students acquire and emulate formulaic language as they move toward constructing longer turns of speech. These would be questions such as:

- Where do students pick up academic speaking phrases in university settings and in what ways?
- Who carries the work of teaching these phrases within a university setting?

We believe the answers to these questions tell us a great deal about teaching our academic speaking courses. We hope you find the consideration of these questions and the course designs presented within this Brief Instructional Guide helpful for your students as well as your teaching practice. We envision this volume to be particularly beneficial to English language instructors in higher education who understand how additional languages are learned.

One of the primary focuses of this Brief Instructional Guide is to show how we contribute to our students' ability to communicate within the greater academic community and within their specific discipline. Communicating effectively can be a difficult task for our students as they engage in a variety of environments on campus. We describe academic speaking in our context as the types of oral acts occurring in our campus community. Academic speaking involves the ways our population verbally communicates complex disciplinary concepts and ideas across differing academic situations. We continue to confirm that they are learning different types of English: the language of the university, academic language, and the language within their disciplines.

Learning lexical phrases in academic speaking is often a precursor to communicative tasks. Following this line of thinking, this Brief Instructional Guide introduces several things, each leading to how we view these phrases as building blocks to learning academic speaking. We start by providing an overview of how these phrases have shaped our language teaching. In revisiting the chapter by Graham and Barone (2001), we offer an overview of formulaic language in academic speaking, how phrases influenced the design of academic speaking courses at our university two decades ago, and what we have learned since. We unpack insights and concepts we've developed from using lexical phrases in teaching academic speaking. We wanted to explore to what extent this existing literature continued to align with and inform our context. In considering our own institutional space, this literature helps us to continue to reflect on and explore ways to improve our practice. We provide brief overviews informed by the campus realities and the complexity of critical thinking within disciplines.

We then move to the section of our primary focus, which provides a description of our course design anchoring to lexical phrases and context, along with tasks that provide students opportunities to practice language chunking in realistic and communicative ways. We discuss how an academic speaking course can supply opportunities for students to think through formulaic phrases and what those phrases mean within their own disciplines. By cultivating this type of critical thinking, we hope this Brief Instructional Guide helps language instructors in higher education contexts rethink academic speaking by going beyond the boundaries of language chunking and helping their students improve their ability to speak more competently and comfortably within academic settings.

We envision this volume as a way for language teachers and program developers to consider how best to meet the needs of their students in their specific contexts where students must orally navigate academic situations and verbalize their complex disciplinary thinking. More broadly, this volume offers any educator—language teacher, educational specialist, university administrator, etc.—a cross-section of what may take place in the language-learning classroom within a university setting.

1. Twenty Years of Teaching Lexical Phrases in Academic Speaking

University students are required to verbally represent themselves in a myriad of academic situations and must find ways to communicate their ideas and dialogue accurately and effectively with others daily. There are multiple places graduate and professional students are required to present themselves through spoken language—from classroom discussions and debates to presentations and oral doctoral defenses.

Because we find that our students are required to engage in these and other academically oriented situations, our university's English Language Center (ELC) developed an English for Academic Purposes (EAP) Academic Speaking course to help students and scholars who use English as an Additional Language (EAL) succeed in this competitive R1 academic context. How we view and support the internationalization of our university was thoroughly mapped out and informed by the use of the EAP approach in our courses.

What informs the design and continued development of our Academic Speaking course is an understanding that academic speaking involves a variety of communicative acts: language, gesturing, timing, engagement with audience, prosody, etc. Additionally, our students find themselves needing to verbalize their ideas spontaneously rather than in structured presentations. Importantly, these linguistic demands require them to use language to express complex thoughts.

While there are many ways of designing academic speaking courses, especially those designed for multidisciplinary audiences, we generally concentrate on the varied ways students can practice communicating in academic contexts that simulate panel discussions, role-plays, and video-recordings with Q&A and instructor feedback, and other opportunities for spontaneous speech practice.

In 2001, in the book *Understanding the Courses We Teach*, Graham and Barone outlined an academic speaking course designed to improve the intelligibility of speakers in academic contexts. By describing the institutional setting, conceptual framework, course content, and instructional approaches, they provided teachers of English with ways of designing and implementing a course that would improve students' oral competency in academic situations. They offered strategies for helping students produce academic speech more automatically and with more confidence. In their chapter, "Academic Speaking: Learning to Take 'Longer Turns,'" they suggested that lexical phrases or chunks of language such as those noted in the introduction can assist language learners in the various complex and lengthy "longer turns" of academic conversations that come within the array of academic speaking settings—labs, classrooms, seminars, conferences, and so forth.

Over the last two decades, we have continued to learn that students acquiring chunks of language, specifically discipline-specific language chunks, can foster oral competency and confidence. We have also learned about the varied ways our courses operate within academic institutions and how course design and infrastructure contribute to students' ability to speak intelligibly and confidently in academic settings and transfer those skills across institutional settings.

With this Brief Instructional Guide, we (Barone and Dickinson) revisit the teaching of lexical phrases common in academic speech in current iterations of the course, which has continued to focus specifically on how EALs communicate in academic settings. We continue to see that learning language phrases increases student communicative ability, yet it may remain challenging for students to convey complex, disciplinary-specific ideas that require the use of these set language phrases. Additionally, we have continued to learn about the structural realities and constraints of academic settings. By revisiting the ways instructors have modified, and at times challenged, the generalizability of formulaic language phrases, we continue to view academic phrases as launching points instead of end points as a foundation from which students can reflect on the markers inherent to communication.

The concept of a lexical phrase was first discussed in 1975 by Joseph Becker through the perspective that we speak "mostly by stitching together swatches of text that we have heard before" (p. 1). He believed that knowing a language meant a speaker understands the use of certain phrases in the language. The term "lexical bundle," consequently, was first used in a research-based chapter on the most recurrent sequences in conversation and academic prose (Biber et al., 1999, chap. 13). The term continued to be used over the next decade (see Biber et al., 2004; Partington et al., 2004). The study of phrases is "a fuzzy part of language" (Altenberg, 1998, p. 101), and a multitude of terminology and definitions can be found in the literature on phraseological topics.

In their investigation of lexical bundles in spoken conversation, Biber et al. (1999) found that there are several multi-word combinations, such as (the value) "is going to be" and "what we're going to" in their data (p. 993). Biber et al. (1999), along with Biber and Barbieri (2007), continue using the term, "lexical bundles are pervasive in spoken and written texts, where they serve basic discourse functions related to the expression of stance, discourse organization, and referential framing" (p. 265) when exploring the phrases common in university speaking.

We take a similar approach to groups of words in academic speaking. These common, recurring words offer insight into how discourse occurs in an academic setting. For us, a lexical approach to academic speaking relies on adopting these types of language widely accepted in the field of TESOL: words (such as *way*), chunks that may be fixed phrases (such as *by the way*), and semi-fixed phrases (such as *on the way* or *on my way*) (Thornbury, 2019).

Revisiting Lexical Phrases in Our Institutional Context

In this section, we revisit the original chapter by noting which aspects of an academic speaking course have continued and appear similar today, such as describing methods and commentating on data, and acknowledging those areas that have required updating and changes, such as new technologies, equipment, and processes.

As institutional context, our English Language Center provides language instruction to individuals who use EAL, and the vast majority of our EAP students elect to enroll in our courses to enhance their spoken English. Our instructors are applied linguists and EAP practitioners who focus on the real-world English language needs of the university community. This means our instructors bring a range of educational and teaching backgrounds, coming with experience in international teaching, second-language acquisition, language corpora, and sociolinguistics, to name a few. Individually and collectively, we reflect on our course design, program needs, and materials development on a regular basis.

As applied linguists, we view EAP as "the area of inquiry and practice in the development of language programs for people who need a language to meet a predictable range of communicative needs" (Swales, 1992, p. 300). We view needs analysis as our primary tool of understanding our students' language needs. The needs analysis offers students the opportunity to provide feedback on their understanding of themselves as language learners as well as their perceived language needs. Additionally, the needs analysis informs our course design and practice of engaging in conversations with faculty, deans, and directors. We also draw from our collective experiences, EAP literature, and tools developed during that time.

Graham and Barone defined academic speaking as "the type of speaking that characteristically takes place in the classroom during instruction, in the science lab, in the seminar, or at a scholarly conference" (p. 414). In their conceptualization of their academic speaking course, learning chunks of language used in academic speaking can help students navigate complex academic discourses. Their concept of lengthy academic discourse was rooted in Brown and Yule's (1983) *extended discourse* or *longer turns*. In this view, longer turns, or "[e]xtended discourse consists of utterances of more than just one or two sentences and tends to be transactional, rather than interactional" (Graham & Barone, 2001, p. 412). Possibly one of the most important concepts in understanding how to teach preset chunks of language is that learning shorter chunks of language does not lead to the ability to discourse in situations that require longer turns. In their context, "students who can converse competently in 'short turns' often fail to produce clear and comprehensible longer stretches of discourse" (p. 412). Therefore, teaching longer stretches of language furthers a learner's ability to navigate the different occasions when they must verbally communicate their thoughts within their field.

Graham and Barone's chapter also highlighted ways "of maintaining a *balance* between accuracy and fluency concerns" by encouraging the learner's self-monitoring confidence and teaching these longer turns of conventional formulaic constructions (p. 409). Students may gain more confidence and be more attuned to other aspects of academic speaking (pacing, rhythm, etc.) when they have learned specific phrases to use within academic speaking contexts. Because of this, the authors relied on previous concepts of balance (Harmer, 1991) and designed their course "between activities designed to foster fluency and those designed to foster accuracy" (p. 413).

The academic speaking course described was tailored to their students. The course was geared toward graduate and professional students and international teaching assistants who often find themselves interacting with peers in courses and conducting research at labs. Given the types of speaking acts these students used, their chapter described how important it is to teach ways to produce longer stretches of language to engage in communicative practices. In other words, students often engage in long stretches of discourse, and this type of longer turn is challenging for instructors to teach and for students to learn and acquire.

Students participate in this course for a variety of reasons. Mainly, learners understand the demands of communicating research and disciplinary information throughout campus and throughout their academic careers. Graham and Barone designed their course around the types of communicative acts: the occasions when learners need to verbalize their ideas. For example, students often need to prepare (1) to make presentations in graduate seminars, (2) to defend dissertations, (3) to give papers at scholarly conferences, or (4) to make presentations as part of job interviews.

The course had several features that remain intact today. By design, academic speaking was offered as a 12-week course meeting twice a week for 90-minute sessions with roughly 12 students per course section. This pace allowed for consistent in-class time for their active participation and feedback as well as time between classes for preparation and one-to-one meetings with instructors to receive highly detailed, individualized feedback on their academic speaking skills.

The syllabus focused on five specific areas: lexical phrases, pronunciation, intercultural competencies, communication skills, and presentation skills. We would like to highlight one specific passage in the original chapter that states Graham and Barone's approach to give readers a sense of how the authors viewed the course:

> The approach is layered: for example, we will use certain phrases, such as those for explaining cause and effect (e.g., *X brings about/results in* and *It has nothing to do with X but rather*), as the linguistic content to perform a language function (explaining cause and effect) and then practice performing the language and function through communicative activities. (p. 415)

Students had extensive English language backgrounds and, for many, rather advanced proficiency. It is important to note that these students came from a wide range of disciplines (engineering, chemistry, social sciences, etc.). They also came from a variety of language backgrounds and English was an additional language.

Overall, the course was meant to assist international graduate and professional students to adapt to U.S. academic communicative contexts and improve their ability to effectively verbalize their ideas. The original chapter offered several key takeaways. We take time here to briefly describe the key features of Graham and Barone's chapter with an understanding that if readers want a highly detailed description, they can access the original chapter for its comprehensive description of the course.

Graham and Barone based their course design on an understanding of Robinson's (1980) EAP model, which challenges EAP courses to revolve around a goal other than language competence and to be infused with the needs of the learners in context.

They discussed an important conceptual understanding of these phrases that they specifically had woven throughout the design of their course. They use in their chapter Nattinger and DeCarrico's (1992) definition of lexical phrases, as "prefabricated, formulaic, and conventional." To Graham and Barone in 2001, "[m]emorized lexical phrases can, with practice, become automatic, thus significantly lowering cognitive load, and freeing a speaker's mind to think about the ideas requiring expression and to focus on self-monitoring their speech" (p. 412).

For the most part, Graham and Barone focused on building lexical phrase use by practice through role-plays, presentations, debates, and roundtable discussions. Grounding lexical phrases in these types of tasks enabled students to engage in authentic and realistic communicative contexts. For Graham and Barone, teaching these phrases in longer turns allowed instructors to engage students in the language of numbers, description, process, cause and effect, discourse signaling, among other language functions. Their chapter (the appendix specifically) listed several longer phrases that students might use within their own disciplinary context. In the activities they presented, memorizing and practicing phrases is part of the process of retaining and using them. While the course used a variety of methods for teaching phrases, there was an understanding that students should learn and practice them with content from their discipline, prepare a brief presentation on a topic from their discipline using them, and learn ways to identify phrases inside their discipline, etc.

In this updated volume, Barone and Dickinson highlight how students must continually balance their language choices in their academic speaking with campus realities, disciplinary demands, and social encounters. In other words, students must learn how to situate these phrases in the broader academic context.

2. Concepts and Insights for Lexical Phrases in Teaching Academic Speaking

We start this next section by briefly revisiting our conceptual understanding of academic speaking in our context. On a competitive R1 campus with over a thousand speakers of multiple languages, our students discourse in a variety of complex settings daily—working in labs, listening to lectures, participating in discussions and debates, and presenting their research—so there is a constant demand for instruction to improve how students communicate. In our view, there is a lot at stake for our students as they navigate through their academic programs.

Because of this range of language needs, we have a broad perspective on what constitutes academic speaking, which for us includes the types of tasks on campus where a student needs to verbally communicate their ideas to another individual or group. We see speaking tasks such as small, informal group discussions to formal dissertation defenses as both building a student's knowledge base as well as enculturating a student into their discipline's way of speaking (Casanave, 2002). Academic speaking generally takes place in a shared context where communication is interactive and in real time in a range of registers depending on the context and genre. Our definition aligns with Granger's (2009) explanation that phraseology looks at the "continuous contextualized discourse" uttered by individuals (p. 16). How lexical phrases are approached and what constitutes a lexical phrase lies at a crossroads between an individual's theoretical and methodological preferences in research. We want to keep our definition broad enough to include the spontaneous speech acts our students engage in on campus and the characteristics of those acts.

Graham and Barone's original chapter chose to focus on the role and benefit of a lexical approach at a time when academic speaking corpora were emerging as tools to inform their course design. We want to call attention to other dynamics happening within our Academic Speaking course over the last 20 years, offering new insight into an already complex course. With this in mind, we address other elements that the original chapter did not have scope and space to address.

Through a lexical approach, students learn the linguistic function of various chunks of language. We still find this valuable. We also find other aspects of teaching lexical phrases valuable. Our insights into our courses reveal that student choice and critical thinking are key elements occurring when students verbalize complex ideas. For instance, the ways they exhibit choice and verbally communicate complex ideas with these phrases demonstrates how linguistic and cognitive engagement often surfaces. Through this linguistic and cognitive engagement, we find students to be actively adapting their language and practicing and negotiating language use, signaling affective and pragmatic awareness.

In speaking activities, there are signs of cognitive and affective engagement between and among students, with the instructor, and collectively. A student's linguistic competence and practice often interplays with their audience awareness. Using lexical phrases in communicating complex ideas also requires them to adapt when an audience or listener cannot track the information they are hearing. Using these phrases is part linguistic and part prosody and includes a demonstration of being able to express intonation and tone that matches the context. In considering the range and types of registers a person uses each day and how these registers can vary greatly depending on campus expectations and population, students learn to make linguistic choices based on a need for adaptability, indeterminacy, and salience in communicative acts (Balconi & Amenta, 2010). These communication strategies are both challenging to teach and take time to learn. Yet, in our view, most communicative acts are combinations of linguistic (lexical in this case), pragmatic, affective, and cognitive factors. In other words, we see linguistic, cognitive, and affective engagement as requirements for achieving a level of linguistic and pragmatic competence.

Many of our students are highly trained in specialized areas. Daily, they engage with researchers, professors, and classmates, discussing their field of study. With global competitiveness and access to R1 research resources, they often come to academic speaking knowing and having completed original and/or empirical research of some type. Students are balancing the specificity of the language in their field along with the rhetorical purpose of language chunks used in many disciplines. Knowing the language of their field involves knowledge of both lexical phrases common in academic speaking at a university and the language common in their field.

Critical thinking is a complex activity evaluated in a variety of ways. There is no denying that some form of critical thinking occurs when our students balance prefabricated language chunks with their own choice of how to use lexical phrases rhetorically when verbalizing their complex ideas. Our Academic Speaking course tends to approach their verbalization of complex ideas as deeply layered critical thinking (Atkinson, 1997). Making constant choices in language use is one way our students conceptualize their discipline and the complex thoughts within it.

Furthermore, when teaching lexical phrases in communicative tasks, we find it helpful to look at the social function of the lexical phrase and task. This helps us consider the ways academic speaking environments are shaped by social factors, which are ever-changing and often difficult to describe to students. We provide a detailed explanation of how we approach this type of language in the following lesson particulars section which provides a snapshot of the lessons in our course.

Controversies occur often within disciplines as researchers form new models, theories, opinions, etc. We find it is beneficial to explore the affective nature of specific lexical phrases in situations where students might be confronted with controversies within their field. We also spend time looking at the affective use of phrases in situations where students must do other types of communicating: talking with feeling, using language to express emotion or confidence, and communicating their feelings on a subject. We provide a detailed explanation in the lesson particulars section of how this can be approached.

Course Design

Based on our historical perspective, we find it valuable to review both how we approach the course and how we view lexical phrases within the course. Shortly after Graham and Barone's chapter, the literature continued to suggest the high level of importance of teaching phrases to students—phrases that would become part of their communicative acts. It was clear that language was made of a series of words. Wray (2002) noted, "Words belong with other words not as an afterthought but at the most fundamental level" (p. 13). Knowing this information, the challenge continues to be how to identify the phrases that most commonly exist in academic settings and are tied to specific speaking tasks in a certain register. We have engaged in carefully reviewing studies which help us determine just that: which phrases occur when, and in which register, context, and genre. These studies focus primarily on two different types of research: descriptive corpus and usage-based studies. Both types help identify patterns of words and determine the types of phrases we provide.

The way our curriculum incorporates these phrases into academic speaking courses revolves around a series of choices by the instructors that focus on how they would like to engage their students in learning lexical phrases toward the goal of using longer turns. We select phrases that focus on authentic language acts and generally select studies on language conducted using methodologies that provide context-driven data. When authentic speech is collected, the data produced can inform our understanding of the phrases being used and allow us to see how and where pauses and false starts may be considered parts of discourse rather than errors (Aijmer, 2011, p. 232).

In creating course content, we avoid simply providing students with long lists of phrases, which may overwhelm them and not convey meaning. Instead, we provide a select number of phrases that focus on longer turns—longer phrases that can support students in mastering sufficiently sizable lexical phrases. Mastering sufficiently sizable phrases is one of the characteristics of advanced proficiency in a second language (Durrant & Schmitt, 2009; Granger & Bestgen, 2014), and without exposure to the target language, learners tend to be slow at phrasal competence (Forsberg, 2010; Li & Schmitt, 2009).

Some of our instructors directly incorporate corpora into their teaching activities or lessons, gaining insights into the types of language used within speaking tasks. While the number of corpus studies in writing far outweighs the number in speaking, we still find it helpful to note that corpora have and will inform the content and design of our courses for the foreseeable future.

As mentioned earlier, there is not one inclusive list of lexical phrases in spoken university registers, and we find that phrases occur in varied speaking contexts. Biber and Barbieri (2007) looked at a wide range of communicative acts on campus, determining that lexical bundles are more common in non-academic university registers than in instructional registers. Therefore, the types of phrases we provide need to be context-specific and reflect the types of environments in which our students engage. Given the multidisciplinary nature and the different needs of our students, a needs-analysis approach helps us choose lexical phrases that are evidenced in the literature while also teaching phrases they need in their unique contexts. In other words, our phrase lists are often research based, context driven, and needs based.

After the process of selecting longer lexical phrases, we consider the various ways to teach these phrases. Eyckmans et al. (2016), and others, are among those on an "ongoing quest for ways to engage learners in the kinds of processing likely to help them durably entrench lexical phrases in memory" (p. 128). Retaining these phrases is a difficult and complex process, especially since it does not simply occur by rote memorization or workbook-style activities.

We have learned key aspects about teaching lexical phrases that we purposefully focus on, such as how important it is for students to identify them in texts themselves (Jones & Haywood, 2004) and how useful web-based resources can be (Chen, 2011). When students search for phrases and evaluate meaning, they learn better (Laufer & Hulstijn, 2001), and using online resources to search for them decreases the amount of time spent finding and locating such phrases. While deliberate study alone will not allow the acquisition of all phrases (Nation, 2013, p. 92), presenting students with sets of preselected phrases for deliberate study can help (Webb & Kagimoto, 2011). We are strategic with the types of phrases our students are exposed to and when (as explained further on).

Our instructors focus on the types of tasks our students either encounter most frequently or for which they need the most assistance. When designing courses, we have historically drawn from four major sources: available research, textbooks, classroom observations, and other resources (e.g., the lexical syllabus in Willis & Willis, 2012). The last 20 years of using lexical phrases as a primary tool for teaching academic speaking has informed us of a considerable volume of information, phrase lists, and course design options. While we discuss specific literature and textbooks within this text, we do not attempt to cover the vast publications related to lexical phrases. Instead, we choose to focus on the genre of the resource and how we take up those resources.

We start by reading a wide range of literature related to lexical phrase use and then select literature that gives us insight into major shifts that affect our students. We seek out a range of resources (textbooks, literature, curriculum, handbooks, etc.) that can provide us insight into common language phrases, whether discipline-specific or task-specific, with each type of resource adding to our understanding of how academic speaking courses can be built and taught. Each resource informs how lexical phrases impact language acquisition and disciplinary development. We explain in this section how we take up the resources available to us.

We find that no single textbook can meet the demands of our student population. Some of the activities and content of textbooks may not provide our students with examples of what they are experiencing in their communicative acts within the university setting. However, we are also fully aware that to ignore the use of any textbooks would leave our students lacking. Therefore, we seek to choose selections and excerpts from textbooks which provide examples of authentic lexical phrase use that align with the types of language tasks we have identified that our students may need to use. This view seems to be supported by the literature that shows how commercially produced language teaching textbooks do not present pragmatically authentic models of language and discourse (see Bardovi-Harlig et al., 2015). On the other side of this discussion, we understand that studies on lexical phrases, while extremely helpful to our understanding of what phrases are used and at what frequency, might lack direct pedagogical implications of curriculum design.

With updated and more advanced corpora and other related tools currently available, our thoughts regarding the possibilities of teaching lexical phrases in classrooms have moved toward teaching common task-based phrases in university registers, teaching discipline-specific language, and strategically exposing students to authentic spoken registers.

Long before Graham and Barone's chapter, we saw textbooks such as *Academically Speaking* by Kayfetz and Stice (1987) helpful in building courses focused on lexical phrases in higher education. This textbook includes selected "useful expressions" as they referenced them in each chapter throughout the text. These are phrases that can help students complete a myriad of speaking tasks, such as interpreting graphs, defining terms, defending a position, and discussing information, to name a few. Although published over 30 years ago, we find this type of historical volume still highly relevant to the types of tasks students are asked to complete. The types of phrases and activities included within Kayfetz and Stice's work still contribute to our students' understanding of lexical phrase use within their university setting. The phrases revolve around common American college campus speaking interactions and tasks. While helpful, this type of textbook had a limited selection of phrases for five or six specific types of interactions. Further, similar to the limitations of many texts, this textbook did not address how these phrases are situated into the broader academic context.

Another historical text, *Functions of American English* by Jones and von Baeyer (1983), covers a wide range of different speaking tasks (called language functions in their book). While the content focuses on daily interactions for students, they need activities that can be used within their university environment. Because of this particular need, we find Jones and Baeyer's activities on giving presentations, persuading an audience, and talking about differences extremely helpful to practice (see pp. 34, 56, 64). These sections of the textbook have phrases which can help students express complicated concepts such as probability and affirming objections.

For more lists of lexical phrases in given speaking tasks, see *Discussion and Interaction in the Academic Community* by Madden and Rohlck (1997, pp. 47–51, 56–60). First published in 1998, Kehe and Kehe's *Discussion Strategies: Beyond Everyday Conversation* has multiple lists of "helpful expressions" throughout the text that we find relevant to our students' needs. In this text, you will find smaller (and therefore more manageable) lists, specifically for helping discussion leaders, interrupting the floor, asking for clarification, and expressions for agreement/disagreement, along with several others.

We view these texts as providing relevant lexical phrases while also allowing for our own adaptation for our students and context. However, with the ever-changing demands and institutional needs, we find it necessary to constantly reflect on new ways we can use the resources available to us and search for new resources which meet our current students' needs. With these examples, we hope the reader acknowledges with us that there is beneficial historical understanding and resources that can inform our more current understanding of how academic language may be acquired as academic identities are constructed.

Our syllabus is divided into tasks or types of communicative acts, which can be accomplished in multiple ways. Given our relatively limited time with students, our courses must focus on the types of tasks they either encounter the most or those with which they need the most assistance. This section focuses on how the EAP approach of needs analysis, and our experiences, along with research and tools that have developed over time, inform how we now take up the resources we currently have available to us.

We have not found a text that fully addresses how to use lexical phrases in a multidisciplinary space that also addresses students' need to discover particular phrases related to their disciplines. In designing our course, we rely on an array of textbooks, some of which are cornerstone books for how academic speaking has been seen throughout the years, while others which are recent contributions to the educational textbook market. We see many books providing us with content that our students can and have learned from over the years.

A representation of the literature supports and challenges how often the phrases in some textbooks are used in speaking contexts (Biber et al., 2004). However, we take the approach that textbooks offer us opportunities to reconsider and rethink what fits in our contexts. Reading textbooks in critically affirming ways can help us understand how our courses fit in the larger scheme of academic speaking on university campuses.

Some textbooks have more recently become discipline-specific—as we continue to document the language of specific fields, through classroom observations and corpus analysis. We often pull from these texts to keep our students aware that academic language learning, especially at the graduate level, is in part learning U.S. English as well as learning the language of the discipline. To simplify, some disciplines discuss statistics, numbers, graphs, and charts more often than others (science versus divinity, for example). While that is a generalized statement, we find it tends to be true in our courses as students describe the types of communicative acts happening within their schools. Given that our courses are multidisciplinary, we attempt to provide supplemental resources that might help them acquire more language phrases within their field. While not organized based on lexical phrases specifically, texts such as *English for Science and Engineering* by Ivor Williams (2007) provides us with disciplinary-specific activities and examples of language for some of our students. This example gives us authentic and relevant scenarios for speaking tasks for engineers and walks students through the types of responses one might give. While the text is not focused on lists of phrases, these activities are easily adaptable to our context, given one goal of our course is to provide authentic speaking practice for real-life communicative acts outside of class. Our point is that both historical textbooks and recently published textbooks can build a course that is relevant to students' needs.

3. Rethinking Longer Turns in Academic Speaking

In this section, we begin with the core aspect of our courses, the use of lexical phrases, and move toward other aspects such as social function, student choice and adaptability, and critical thinking, among others. Finally, we provide a few reflections on the day-to-day lesson particulars by showing how two communicative acts—interrupting and holding the floor as well as expressing opinions—are approached with these varying aspects in mind.

Going Beyond the Boundaries of Lexical Phrases

Since our context is multidisciplinary, we primarily focus on lexical phrases that are found across disciplines, such as *to begin with*, and identify how the represented disciplines take up common phrases, for example, some use the phrase *the x axis represents...* while others do not. We find it helpful to review and update the phrases we teach, so we consistently reexamine new lexical phrase lists related to academic language. We also base our course content on student feedback on their linguistic needs and course resources, while also drawing from the disciplines and university contexts. Because of the more advanced digital tools available to use now—corpora and concordances, online self-study materials, and a growing list of publications—we are better able to show students ways to access lexical phrases and strategies for applying this information to their academic language development.

As a specific example of this approach, we offer students a lesson introducing the language of presenting overviews, which we briefly describe in the following section.

Useful Language for Overviews

My presentation is in three parts.
My presentation is divided into three main sections.

Today, I'm going to
take a look at ...
talk about ...
examine ...
tell you something about the background ...
give you some facts and figures ...
fill you in on the history of ...
concentrate on ...
limit myself to the question of ...

We might begin by discussing the nuances of each longer turn (i.e., comparing *talk about* to *concentrate on*). We want students to become familiar with lexical phrases and comfortable navigating them, which can spark interest in their own corpus exploration of phrases. Next, we might focus on the social functions of each phrase and begin discussing the disciplinary expectations of a particular language phrase, aspects which potentially offer students control over the language they choose to use.

In the original chapter, the academic lexical phrases in the syllabus were predetermined. These lists came from existing data in textbooks and literature and were where Graham and Barone found disciplinary language had overlaps in multiple disciplines. Students were encouraged to learn phrases the instructor had preselected, which were suitable for a class representing a range of disciplines. Additionally, the instructors would draw students' attention to the approach of learning these phrases for the purpose of using them in their disciplinary areas.

During this course, lexical phrases were introduced to students through communicative tasks. Instructors introduced specific phrases, explaining and contextualizing their function and modeling their pronunciation. As an example, students needed to verbalize numbers or describe objects, and they might discuss the purpose of these types of phrases as they related to presenting their research:

1. **Verbalizing numbers and mathematics**
   Examples: a is to b as c is to d
   X divided by Y equals
   plus or minus (number)
2. **Describing objects—shape, size, amount, orientation, location**
   Examples: X is ______ in height and ______ in width.
   close together / far apart
   in the upper/lower right-hand / left-hand corner

3. **Explaining research: purpose, results, graphs, tables**
   Examples: the purpose of this research/study/investigation was to determine
   the results seem to show/suggest that
   the x/y axis represents

After learning these phrases, students participated in simulated academic speaking situations for practice and use. They were then given an opportunity to explore phrases within the specific areas of their discipline and to tie them to content from their own fields of study. To illustrate this approach, we provide an excerpt below. This excerpt provides a general description of how instructors would use phrases to cultivate student engagement and critical thinking.

> Excerpt from 2001 chapter
>
> First, we introduce the phrases to be studied, explaining their function and modeling their pronunciation. We try to establish the importance of being able to use such phrases fluently and accurately. Our initial activities may be structured, but we attempt to create and simulate realistic, relevant contexts and situations so that students can use the phrases aptly and meaningfully. We ask students to construct sentences tied to content from their fields of specialization. At this early presentation and practice stage, we often provide images and other graphics, such as charts and tables as a way into more communicative tasks. (p. 416)

Through this excerpt, we can see that instructors valued the linguistic attributes of longer stretches of discourse by having students listen for features that might hinder the audience's ability to understand their meaning. As we have mentioned, the original chapter focused primarily on the linguistic aspects of teaching lexical phrases. We now explore other aspects that have emerged when teaching academic speaking through the use of these phrases.

Student Choice, Critical Thinking, and Adaptive Lexical Phrase Use

Writing this volume has given us time to reflect on how we currently approach this course, particularly on how students interact with lexical phrase lists as they engage with content from their discipline. We have explored ways in which critical thinking can occur when students are exposed to and practice verbalizing complex ideas by learning common phrases within their discipline. Here, we reflect on the ways they negotiate and select the types of phrases they prefer to use when verbalizing their ideas, while adhering to disciplinary demands and expectations of language use.

As an example, our students often need to describe their projects. Whether in classroom settings, conference presentations, or master's/doctoral defenses, our students need to find ways to communicate about their academic work and need to choose suitable language to verbalize what they have accomplished and how they achieved it.

Many decisions regarding course content are based on at least two specific elements that occur within the first week of class: the pre-needs analysis our students complete before our course and the types of disciplines represented. Since our courses are multidisciplinary, we may have a wide range of students, which is why a needs analysis is extremely helpful in determining content. We find that our speaking courses differ from our writing courses in that they demand a different approach to identifying content, especially considering that the type of spoken communication acts needed must be adapted to different audiences and tasks. Identifying writing content requires language that adapts more specifically to the same audiences, such as a dissertation committee or an academic journal. We consistently have students listen to speakers in their field, record lectures by key professors in their discipline, and borrow certain phrases from texts published in their discipline.

During our semester, we provide students with two to three individual meetings where the student meets with the instructor to review speaking skills, receive personalized instruction, and discuss ways to work on what they find challenging in the course. In these meetings, students discuss their use of lexical phrases and their choices about the types of phrases they feel comfortable using. We find these individual meetings are helpful places to elicit feedback and encourage conversations with students on their perceptions and understandings of lexical phrases and phrase lists.

We also find our students benefit from multiple uses of corpora and academic phrase banks as they seek authentic language. We provide them with tutorials on available corpus-related tools if they choose this approach. Some find it helpful to see how often phrases are used compared to others. We might briefly explain the role of a corpus and what it may or may not tell us. Then we might show two different lexical phrases and compare the results in a corpus to help students critically think through the differences between the phrases. For example, we may prompt them to search for the following two phrases: *sorry to interrupt* versus *could you repeat that?* Discussing and critically thinking through the differences between these two phrases might show students how important it can be to "interrupt" a speaker when the listener does not understand the point being made. Rather than waiting until the speaker has fully completed their speaking, it might be better in some situations to save the speaker time and have them clarify throughout the conversation. Using a corpus supports these types of important conversations with students.

We consistently offer students opportunities to engage in activities that require a certain level of adaptive and flexible use of lexical phrases. Activities such as turn-taking, group discussions, and exploring cultural differences provide opportunities for students to think through how commonly these phrases might be combined with other language devices such as hedging (using words such as *might* or *could* or *may*) or boosting.

Our students practice how to adapt to varying academic contexts, audiences, and interlocutors. For example, a student may need to repeatedly use phrases to help clarify and refine their understanding. In this case, the student might use a phrase such as *if I understood you correctly, you mean* ____ or *What exactly do you mean by that?* However, if the student's lexical phrase repertoire is limited and they find themselves constantly repeating these phrases without flexibility and variation, then the listener's attention may focus on the language as "fixed," which can sometimes disrupt the flow of communication. Therefore, having students think through strategies for these and other scenarios that occur in group discussions helps them both to use these phrases and to adapt their usage. We find that communicative acts such as group discussions and turn-taking require learning the lexical phrases along with strategies for adjusting to the tone of the group discussion/conversation by adapting and being flexible during the conversation. Of course, this takes a certain level of language proficiency, practice, and confidence.

Lesson Particulars

Next, it is helpful to provide another type of snapshot of our Academic Speaking course. The following is a description of a class that reviews a set of lexical phrases and provides progressively less structured and more extemporaneous practice opportunities. In some ways, our context and university atmosphere are drastically different compared to 2001 by virtue of technological developments and campus initiatives related to diversity, equity, and inclusion. However, in many ways, overlapping academic language across disciplines is not much different from the type of language students will produce in their disciplinary contexts. In fact, the course description, objectives, and weekly themes found in the course syllabus are derivative of earlier iterations of the course and remain relevant. The following lesson particulars focusing on the phrases associated with *interrupting and holding the floor* is situated in the third week of class. This same class session includes attention to Intercultural Communication (Part 2 from the previous week) and is contained in the context of Leading and Participating in a Group Discussion.

Interrupting and holding the floor is a type of communicative act that occurs daily for many of our students. Whether in group discussions (in classes, labs, research teams, etc.), in student–professor interactions, or in attending campus seminars and guest speakers, students find themselves in situations that require what is often called "turn-taking" or "interrupting and holding the floor."

We offer a common list of lexical phrases informed by the Michigan Corpus of Academic Spoken English (MICASE) and other resources and textbooks on common phrases in group discussions:

Could you repeat that, please?
Sorry to interrupt, but ...
I didn't get/catch that.
I wonder if you could explain ...
May I interrupt for a moment ...
Do you mind if I say something?

When teaching interactional types of communicative tasks, we find it helpful to look first at the social function of the task. In this instance, we find it valuable to discuss how "interrupting" is viewed culturally as well as across disciplines and specific settings. Do we observe students interrupting in different ways during an engineering lecture as compared to an educational theory class, and if so, how do they differ? In what ways is interrupting perceived by other students or the professor? Does it depend on the atmosphere of the class? Who is teaching the course, how many students are in the course, and what is the level of students in the course? These types of questions prompt our students to consider the ways academic speaking environments are shaped by social factors. In other words, the social environment in one class might be quite different from the social environment in another class.

Students must also consider the affective aspects of their linguistic use—the lexical phrases they choose to use and when—in the discussion.

For example, saying *Could you repeat that?* or *I didn't catch that* requires less of a response from the speaker. Both signal that the speaker must explain the last comment and then potentially move on. Other statements, such as *Sorry to interrupt, but* or *May I interrupt for a moment*, can signal something much different to the speaker. Depending on the speaker and context, when an audience member says these phrases, the speaker may assume the audience member disagrees with a statement or is about to disagree with them. Having students consider what the word *interrupt* can mean in different contexts and disciplines can help them think critically about when and how often to use such a phrase.

For our purposes, we use the concept of affective use to mean the difference between what someone is saying compared to the inflection used while saying the lexical phrase. Instructors may pause within the lesson to discuss the different ways speakers can use thought-groups, intonation, and word stress with these phrases. For example, an instructor might discuss the difference between these two particular uses of thought-groups:

May I // interrupt for a moment
May I interrupt // for a moment

Students can consider the differences between these two pauses and where they occur. Similarly, critical thinking (in terms of adaptability and flexibility) could also be discussed at this point in the lesson. After discussing the implications of using a thought-group pause after *I* or after *interrupt*, students can benefit from examples of when a speaker might adapt their thought-groups depending on the audience. In situations where interrupting might cause a distraction or be seen as a sign of disrespect, a speaker might take a longer pause after *interrupt* to give the listener time to interject. A longer pause can signal to the listener that you respect their time. These examples are context dependent. We are simply suggesting there are opportunities when teaching lexical phrases for speakers to critically think through the options for being adaptable and flexible in situations when they are using them.

In addition, some of our instructors find this time in the lesson to be an opportunity to discuss disciplinary demands or corpus exploration. However, one of the challenges in teaching academic speaking is the lack of authentic Q&A corpora. If we had a variety of this type of corpus, we could have students explore the frequency of these types of phrases for interrupting and how speakers use all the elements we have discussed so far: thought-groups, adaptability, affective considerations, social functions, etc. Instead, we often suggest students consider seeking out an oral mentor—whether formal or informal.

Formal oral mentors can have conversations with students on how these types of phrases are considered in certain situations in their respective fields. That type of relationship is not as common as informal mentors. Informal mentors are mentors that students have identified as "model speakers" in their fields. These informal mentors may not have an actual relationship with our students or know them; however, they may have enough recorded speaking lectures, keynote presentations, and website videos that students can listen to and learn from.

We also offer students multiple opportunities to provide feedback on how confident they are in using lexical phrases, and how likely they are to infuse them into their speaking. These reflections and student feedback are an important feature of the speaking classroom. Communicating feedback allows students to talk about the language they use in ways that other places on campus do not always allow. Our courses offer students spaces to openly reflect on their understanding of the language we discuss.

Course Artifacts

Our Academic Speaking syllabus and pre- and post-needs analysis, which we have provided for you in the Appendix, demonstrate how we view this course. These documents provide another way of seeing how we balance students' needs with course content. Our purpose and goals within the syllabus specifically reflect the insights we have gained. We ground much of our syllabus around the course description, which emphasizes our goal that students learn the lexical phrases and discourse markers necessary for each speaking task as well as compensatory strategies to help them be understood in spite of differences in accent and culture.

We use wording in our course description that allows for instructors to adapt their course content to the demographics of a particular class based on the pre-needs analysis. Our goals, aims, and objectives center around students obtaining the language needed to communicate their own ideas and work within competitive academic settings.

Our courses cover a range of academic speaking aspects. From thinking critically to adapting to audiences to creating meaning with lexical phrases, they highlight all the elements of speaking: linguistic, affective, cognitive, social, and others. We highlight these other elements while continuing to use these phrases as the core component. We have learned that lexical phrases are still crucial to navigating academic communicative acts, as well as all the other elements we also focus on now in our courses.

Future Thinking

Our goal has always been to equip students with the ability to verbalize their academic, professional, and personal ideas in our university setting. We want them to see the benefit of knowing and predicting the type of language they may need in their academic setting and for developing their academic language skills to engage in complex academic inquiry. Toward this end, we continue to understand that lexical phrases are essential linguistic tools.

When considering the future of academic speaking, it is tempting to believe that many of the challenges of language learning can be greatly minimized by new tools. We remain convinced that a core approach—teaching lexical phrases—provides our students with the language needed to communicate their complex thoughts. On the surface, the phrases and types of tasks which appear in our courses seem similar compared to two decades ago. Yet, our way of thinking about and discussing these phrases with students and colleagues now attempts to include the wide array of components of language, which was well beyond the scope of the original chapter. In this Brief Instructional Guide, we have discussed some of these additional components, and we hope by talking through these components, other instructors now have more insight into teaching lexical phrases within their context.

Campus Realities

Every campus should strive toward better understanding how their students' English language competencies are viewed within institutional courses and programs as well as how their English language use is supported or challenged throughout the university. We take a minute here to describe and think through some of the realities of our campus.

In many academic contexts, language is differentiated by new and increased demands on students. Students are increasingly required to present their work earlier in their academic trajectory. It is not uncommon for undergraduates to arrive on campus having completed original research or for graduate students to be published before they graduate. The reality on many campuses is that students are expected to describe and discuss their research, disciplinary content, and/or future research agenda at earlier stages than ever before.

Importantly, our students encounter a number of differing campus entities on a regular basis. Students are often having conversations with their professors, meeting with advisors, and participating in classroom discussions. Participating in communicative acts across campus, students are possibly faced with different views on their reuse of specific language or common phrases since listeners perceive formulaic phrases in various ways (Boers et al., 2006). In some disciplines, stylistic concerns, such as what is perceived as too much repetitive use of transitions (equated with learned formulaic language), may not matter as much as they do in other disciplines. We often reflect on how our students' language use is viewed on campus. The good news is that the students in our courses are using an eclectic range of resources beyond the classroom on campus to increase their ability to verbally communicate their own ideas.

Materials-Light Approach

We would like to take note of the volume and variety of materials and resources students receive related to the academic language they are expected to produce. It is fairly common for our students to acquire materials from various places on campus. A student can be invited to a scientific writing workshop sponsored by the writing studio, a networking workshop for international students sponsored by offices on campus, and a series of graduate student workshops in one semester. In short, students often feel inundated with materials: handouts, links, PowerPoints, resources, etc., some of which may offer contradicting information. What to do with these resources and how much time to spend with each one depending on topic and content are harder questions for students. With handfuls of handouts and resources each term, it is easy for students to feel overwhelmed by the wealth of information provided to them. We see this happening with our language learners as well. With all the available online resources, in-house resources offered by the ELC, and additional supporting resources from other university offices (i.e., the writing center, graduate office, etc.), we have found students can benefit from a clear understanding of what resources they are being given and a prioritization of the materials they receive. Students at advanced levels can sometimes decipher what counts as a critical resource for them and what counts as a supplemental resource for their development as language learners and graduate students. Students who are new to a competitive university setting or students who have difficulty determining what types of materials can assist them might need a different approach when it comes to providing resources to them. We find a materials-light approach is helpful in offering students the type of critical resources they may need for their time at our university while also discussing during class what makes a resource critical for them based on their needs. In class, we might discuss what types of resources they find valuable versus resources they may see as supplemental. These types of conversations allow students to think through what they see as helpful in their language learning, and they also get a chance to hear other students' discussions regarding critical resources.

Using Technologies for Oral Composition

When considering how teaching academic speaking can work alongside new technologies, we anticipate the ways technology use in our courses can support and add to our students' goals while they are at our university. We find the need to balance the type of oral composing with technology our students use on campus with the potential types they will use in their respective fields and careers.

Using technologies in the context of academic speaking extends beyond using slide decks and audio- and video-recordings for formal presentations. The use of corpora and data-driven learning will likely continue, acknowledging that how we use and apply data for pedagogical purposes remains in development and will continue to shape our teaching. More recently, students may need to prepare short, digitally recorded presentations summarizing and promoting their work and participate in virtual conferences. Increasingly, students are gravitating toward individualized instruction using one-to-one consultations. Along these same lines, with so much language-oriented, open-source content and so many language apps and social media groups available, students may further increase the tailoring of their own individualized language instruction.

Using instruction time to teach skills related to using certain types of technology-enhanced presentation software may not be the best use of time with our students, given the time constraints to achieving course objectives and goals as we strive to balance teaching critical aspects of academic speaking with the realities of emerging technologies.

In many ways, then, we return to the same academic speaking space of 20 years ago—continuously asking ourselves how we may better understand what academic speaking is, how our understanding and practice changes over time, and how we may maintain our teaching posture to the benefit of our students. We hope this Brief Instructional Guide has provided a commentary on our perspectives and practices for teaching academic speaking anchored in the teaching of lexical phrases.

APPENDIX

Academic Speaking Syllabus Topics Sample

Course Description

This course offers students an opportunity to improve their academic speaking skills to enhance their experience at Vanderbilt University. Organized around speaking tasks in the U.S. university classroom, this course is highly interactive. Students learn to communicate with classmates, teachers, and general audiences through role-plays, presentations, debates, and discussions. Students learn the lexical phrases and discourse markers necessary for each speaking task as well as compensatory strategies to help them be understood despite differences in accent and culture.

Purpose of Course

This course is designed to help international students, teaching assistants, and any university-affiliated persons with an intermediate to advanced level of spoken English to communicate more effectively in academic settings. Participants will adapt to U.S. academic communication style and become more proficient in presenting their ideas to various audiences.

See the Course Schedule below for topics, concepts, and themes.

Goals

- Increase comprehensibility, fluency, and accuracy
- Improve public speaking skills
- Develop discussion skills
- Improve pronunciation
- Prepare and deliver individual and group (formal and informal) presentations

- Speak in group discussions
- Improve interactional listening skills

Course Schedule

Week 1

- Needs analysis. Personal introductions. Review of objectives for the course. Discussion of personal goals.
- Video-recorded personal narratives or autobiography (~3 minutes).

These sessions will help prepare students to present themselves in a U.S. academic session as well as narrate an event to a group. Emphasis will be on comprehensible speech, organization, and the ability to answer questions. Students will be recorded the first week so that their progress can be observed throughout the semester in other video-recorded sessions.

Week 2

- Intercultural communication (strategy-based)
- Audience and purpose
- Register and body language. Student and teacher roles and interactions

Students will discover similarities and differences in U.S. communication from communication in other countries. As well as being more comfortable in the U.S. with knowledge of general communication habits, students will learn about and use various levels of formality. They will explore teacher and student roles.

Week 3

- Intercultural communication (part 2)
- Leading and participating in a group discussion
- Interrupting and holding the floor

These sessions will show specific aspects of American communication. Students will practice participating in and leading group discussions.

Week 4

- Organizational patterns; discourse markers
- Previews, summaries, main points
- Brainstorming: identifying a problem and offering solutions
- Teamwork

These sessions will prepare students to investigate a problem and work toward solutions. Working in a team, they will learn strategies for achieving goals.

Week 5

- Discuss current events in groups
- Visual aids; charts, tables, and graphs (verbalizing mathematics)
- Practice for video-recorded group activity

These sessions will teach students to discuss topics in the news. Students will prepare to debate topics and discuss issues in groups.

Week 6

- Student participation, group leadership, and turn-taking
- Video-recorded debate or group discussion

These sessions will teach students to work in teams and be group leaders. Students will require teamwork skills useful in a U.S. university. They will learn to motivate, facilitate, and organize a team. The video will serve as a mid-term evaluation tool.

Week 7

- Body language, eye contact, gestures, and facial expressions for individual presentations
- Do they differ and if so, how do they differ from those used in group discussions?

Students will practice the correct way to stand and move, and how to engage the audience and use facial expressions in order to have the most effective impact during a presentation.

Week 8

- Word choice and level of formality for individual presentations
- Review presentation samples

These sessions will enhance students' knowledge of register used in presentations in a U.S. academic environment. By critiquing videos, students will learn to recognize elements of an effective presentation.

Week 9

- Speaking to persuade
- Web resources for presentations
- Evaluating resources found on the web

These sessions will prepare students for web-based research and documentation of oral presentations.

Week 10

- Writing outlines, preparing a presentation: developing the main points
- Preparing effective introductions, transitions, and conclusions

These sessions will prepare students to structure a presentation according to U.S. academic conventions and standards. Students will learn to prepare presentation outlines.

Week 11

- Preparation for final presentations. Using outlines and visual aids
- Practice for video-recorded presentations

These sessions will allow students to show all the progress they have made in presentation skills by preparing to be video-recorded for their final evaluation.

Week 12

- Final video-recorded presentations
- Post-needs analysis

These sessions will allow a final practice of presentation skills, which will be video-recorded, and feedback from classmates and teacher, as well as self-evaluations. Progress and suggestions for more improvement will be noted.

Pre- and Post-Needs Analysis

1. **How often do you speak in English?**

    ____ All the time

    ____ Hourly

    ____ At least once a day

    ____ 2–3 times a week

    ____ Only when called on in class

2. How often do you listen to English outside of class (e.g., listen to the radio, watch television, or talk to friends?)

____ Hourly

____ Several times a day

____ At least once a day

____ 2–3 times a week

____ Weekly

3. What speaking tasks do you think you improved?

	Not applicable	No improvement	Some improvement	Good improvement	Much improvement
Making formal presentations (e.g., for conferences)	1	2	3	4	5
Making in-class presentations	1	2	3	4	5
Participating in group projects	1	2	3	4	5
Talking in class	1	2	3	4	5
Participating in study groups	1	2	3	4	5

4. What spoken language functions do you think you improved?

	Not applicable	No improvement	Some improvement	Good improvement	Much improvement
Saying numbers	1	2	3	4	5
Verbalizing mathematics	1	2	3	4	5
Describing shapes	1	2	3	4	5
Defining terms / concepts	1	2	3	4	5

	Not applicable	No improvement	Some improvement	Good improvement	Much improvement
Using the language of your own discipline	1	2	3	4	5
Explaining a process	1	2	3	4	5
Explaining cause and effect	1	2	3	4	5
Agreeing / disagreeing	1	2	3	4	5

5. What pronunciation issues do you think you improved?

	Not applicable	No improvement	Some improvement	Good improvement	Much improvement
Intonation (e.g., sentence rhythm)	1	2	3	4	5
Specific sounds (e.g., use of *-ed* ending, /b/ vs. /v/)	1	2	3	4	5
Word stress (e.g., how to pronounce individual words)	1	2	3	4	5

6. How many hours per week outside of class did you spend on this class?

____ Over 4 hours

____ 3–4 hours

____ 2–3 hours

____ 1–2 hours

____ Less than 1 hour

7. **What did you learn in this class?**

8. **Which aspects of the course do you consider the strongest and why?**

9. **Which aspects of the course do you consider the weakest and why?**

10. **What specific suggestions would you make to improve the course for future participants?**

REFERENCES

Aijmer, K. (2011). Well I'm not sure I think... The use of *well* by non-native speakers. *International Journal of Corpus Linguistics, 16*(2), 231–254. https://doi.org/10.1075/ijcl.16.2.04aij

Altenberg, B. (1998). On the phraseology of spoken English: The evidence of recurrent word combinations. In A. P. Cowie (Ed.), *Phraseology: Theory, analysis and applications* (pp. 101–122). Oxford, UK: Oxford University Press.

Atkinson, D. (1997). A critical approach to critical thinking in TESOL. *TESOL Quarterly, 31*(1), 71–94.

Balconi, M., & Amenta, S. (2010). From pragmatics to neuropragmatics. In M. Balconi (Ed.), *Neuropsychology of communication* (pp. 93–109). Milan: Springer.

Bardovi-Harlig, K., Mossman, S., & Vellenga, H. E. (2015). Developing corpus-based materials to teach pragmatic routines. *TESOL Journal, 6*(3), 499–526. https://doi.org/10.1002/tesj.177

Becker, J. D. (1975). The phrasal lexicon. In *Proceedings of the 1975 Workshop on Theoretical Issues in Natural Language Processing* (pp. 60–63). Stroudsburg, PA: Association for Computational Linguistics.

Biber, D., & Barbieri, F. (2007). Lexical bundles in university spoken and written registers. *English for Specific Purposes, 26*(3), 263–286. https://doi.org/10.1016/j.esp.2006.08.003

Biber, D., Conrad, S., & Cortes, V. (2004). If you look at...: Lexical bundles in university teaching and textbooks. *Applied Linguistics, 25*(3), 371–405. https://doi.org/10.1093/applin/25.3.371

Biber, D., Johansson, S., Leech, G., Conrad, S., & Finegan, E. (1999). *Longman grammar of spoken and written English*. London, UK: Longman.

Boers, F., Eyckmans, J., Kappel, J., Stengers, H., & Demecheleer, M. (2006). Formulaic sequences and perceived oral proficiency: Putting a lexical approach to the test. *Language Teaching Research, 10*(3), 245–261. https://doi.org/10.1191/1362168806lr195oa

Brown, G., & Yule, G. (1983). *Discourse analysis*. Cambridge, UK: Cambridge University Press.

Casanave, C. (2002). *Writing games: Multicultural case studies of academic literacy practices in higher education*. Mahwah, NJ: Lawrence Erlbaum.

Chen, H. J. H. (2011). Developing and evaluating a web-based collocation retrieval tool for EFL students and teachers. *Computer Assisted Language Learning, 24*(1), 59–76. https://doi.org/10.1080/09588221.2010.526945

Durrant, P., & Schmitt, N. (2009). To what extent do native and non-native writers make use of collocations? *International Review of Applied Linguistics in Language Teaching, 47*(2), 157–177. https://doi.10.1515/iral.2009.007

Eyckmans, J., Boers, F., & Lindstromberg, S. (2016). The impact of imposing processing strategies on L2 learners' deliberate study of lexical phrases. *System, 56*, 127–139. http://dx.doi.org/10.1016/j.system.2015.12.001

Forsberg, F. (2010). Using conventional sequences in L2 French. *International Review of Applied Linguistics in Language Teaching, 48*(1), 25–51. https://doi.org/10.1515/text.1.2000.20.1.29

Graham, J. G., & Barone, S. M. (2001). Academic speaking: Learning to take "longer turns." In J. Murphy & P. Byrd (Eds.), *Understanding the courses we teach: Local perspectives on English language teaching* (pp. 409–428). Ann Arbor: University of Michigan Press.

Granger, S. (2009). The contribution of learner corpora to second language acquisition and foreign language teaching. *Corpora and Language Teaching, 33*, 13–32. https://doi.org/10.1075/scl.33.04gra

Granger, S., & Bestgen, Y. (2014). The use of collocations by intermediate vs. advanced non-native writers: A bigram-based study. *International Review of Applied Linguistics in Language Teaching, 52*(3), 229–252. https://doi.org/10.1515/iral-2014-0011

Harmer, J. (1991). *The practice of English language teaching*. Harlow: Longman.

Jones, L., & von Baeyer, C. (1983). *Functions of American English: Communication activities for the classroom*. Cambridge, UK: Cambridge University Press.

Jones, M., & Haywood, S. (2004). Facilitating the acquisition of formulaic sequences. In N. Schmitt (Ed.), *Formulaic sequences: Acquisition, processing, and use* (pp. 269–300). Amsterdam: John Benjamins.

Kayfetz, J. L., & Stice, R. L. (1987). *Academically speaking*. Boston, MA: Heinle & Heinle.

Kehe, D., & Kehe, P. D. (1998). *Discussion strategies: Beyond everyday conversation*. Brattleboro, VT: Pro Lingua Associates.

Laufer, B., & Hulstijn, J. (2001). Incidental vocabulary acquisition in a second language: The construct of task-induced involvement. *Applied Linguistics, 22*(1), 1–26. https://doi.org/10.1093/applin/22.1.1

Li, J., & Schmitt, N. (2009). The acquisition of lexical phrases in academic writing: A longitudinal case study. *Journal of Second Language Writing, 18*(2), 85–102. https://doi.org/10.1111/j.1467-9922.2010.00621.x

Madden, C. G., & Rohlck, T. N. (1997). *Discussion and interaction in the academic community* (Vol. 1). Ann Arbor: University of Michigan Press.

Murphy, J., & P. Byrd (Eds.) (2001). *Understanding the courses we teach: Local perspectives on English language teaching.* Ann Arbor: University of Michigan Press.

Nation, I. S. P. (2013). *Learning vocabulary in another language* (2nd ed.). Cambridge, UK: Cambridge University Press.

Nattinger, J. R., & DeCarrico, J. S. (1992). *Lexical phrases and language teaching.* Oxford: Oxford University Press.

Partington, A., Morley, J., & Haarman, L. (Eds.) (2004). *Corpora and discourse, a most congruous beast.* Bern: Peter Lang. https://doi.org/10.1093/llc/fqi061

Robinson, P. C. (1980). *ESP (English for specific purposes): The present position.* Oxford: Pergamon Press.

Swales, J. M. (1992). *Genre analysis: English in academic and research settings.* Cambridge, UK: Cambridge University Press.

Thornbury, S. (2019). *Learning language in chunks.* Part of the Cambridge Papers in ELT series. Cambridge, UK: Cambridge University Press. https://www.cambridge.org/elt/blog/wp-content/uploads/2019/10/Learning-Language-in-Chunks.pdf

Webb, S., & Kagimoto, E. (2011). Learning collocations: Do the number of collocates, position of the node word, and synonymy affect learning? *Applied Linguistics* 32(3): 259–276. http://dx.doi.org/10.1017/S0272263100014698

Williams, I. (2007). *English for science and engineering.* Boston, MA: Thomson.

Willis, D., & Willis, J. (2012). Corpus analysis for a lexical syllabus. In C. A. Chapelle (Ed.), *The encyclopedia of applied linguistics.* Hoboken, NJ: Wiley-Blackwell. https://doi.org/10.1002/9781405198431.wbeal0235

Wray, A. (2002). *Formulaic language and the lexicon.* Cambridge, UK: Cambridge University Press.